PAVEL
TCHELITCHEW
DRAWINGS

PAVEL

TCHELITCHEW

DRAWINGS

EDITED BY LINCOLN KIRSTEIN

HACKER ART BOOKS   NEW YORK

1970

First published in
New York, 1947

Reprinted by
Hacker Art Books
New York, 1970

Library of Congress Catalog Card Number 77-116363
SBN: 0-87817-046-4

Note

Of the thousands of drawings made by Pavel Tchelitchew in the last twenty-five years, forty-eight are here reproduced. The choice was limited to those which were felt to enjoy a degree of completeness in themselves. Generally speaking, they may be considered as entities, even though frequently they are studies towards the groundwork of a specific picture. Elements from nearly every drawing will be observed in some one of Tchelitchew's paintings.

Three important sets of drawings have been excluded. A remarkable series of studies of freaks and anomalies of nature, combined with essays in perspective, comprise the skeletal research for his large canvas "Phenomena" (1935-1938). A no less beautiful mass of sketches of children, leaves and leaf-children contain the basis for "Hide and Seek" (*Cache-Cache*: 1940-1942), the extraordinary allegory now in the permanent collection of the Museum of Modern Art, New York City (Mrs. Simon Guggenheim Purchase Fund). Since it is proposed to devote future complete monographs to both of these paintings, the greater part of drawings supporting their composition will be reproduced in them. A third series, drawings made for, or inspired by theatre or ballet, are generally omitted since this portion of Tchelitchew's work has already been extensively reproduced, and the artist considers his stage-designs preparatory rather than final. Illustrations made for books and magazines are also likewise available and could be collected at a future time.

Although Tchelitchew has drawn many portraits, those selected here have been chosen purely for their qualities as draughtsmanship. Some of his finest drawings are in French and English collections, notably in those of Sir Kenneth Clark, Lady Juliet Duff, Mr. Geoffrey Gorer, Mr. Edward James, the Honorable Stephen Tennant, Miss Edith Sitwell and Mr. Peter Watson. Those drawings now in Europe have had to be omitted, since all the plates in this book have been made directly from the originals themselves. They are placed in rough chronological order, but their final position was determined by the proportions of the originals as well as the appropriateness of facing pages.

Special thanks are due the Museum of Modern Art, New York City (Miss Dorothy Miller, Curator of Paintings and Drawings); the Fogg Museum of Harvard University (Miss Agnes Mongan, Keeper of Drawings), and the Wadsworth Athenaeum and Morgan Memorial, Hartford, Connecticut (Mr. Charles Cunningham, Director) for permission to withdraw their drawings for reproduction. James Thrall Soby, author of the Tchelitchew monograph published in conjunction with the one-man show presented by the Museum of Modern Art in 1942, is now revising that distinguished catalogue and has been most helpful with information and advice. Thanks of the artist and editor go to those private collectors who deprived themselves of their treasures so that collotype plates could be made by the experts of the Meriden Gravure Company.

The essay preceding the catalogue of plates results from conversations between artist and editor. Part of the formulation derives from each, but everything in it was prompted by the artist.

On Drawing

Beautiful colors are for sale in the shops on the Rialto, but good drawing can only be fetched from the casket of the artist's talent with patient study and sleepless nights, and it is understood and practiced by few.

TINTORETTO

Draw lines, many lines, from memory or from nature; it is in this way that you will become a good artist. INGRES TO DEGAS

The speech of Western draughtsmanship seems, on its highest levels, set and almost ageless. To be sure, there are national or at least geographical differences, as well as differences of time. A Northern drawing or an early Italian drawing can be distinguished at once from a Mannerist or an Impressionist drawing. But in the dominant styles of representation, and in the great families of influence (at least after the note-books of Leonardo), there is an over-all likeness, a common tongue spoken, like the Latin of the Church or of Medicine. In the complete rendering of the nude, for example, as by Raphael, Ingres and Degas, style almost defies epoch, although the dialects in the language of expression may be as varied as successive generations of plants or flowers, which give birth to their own mutations,—which exist in descent, from century to century, but which form parallel, or almost identical types in the Jesse-tree of their tradition. When a new means of rendering emerges, as it infrequently does, means in our own time developed by van Gogh, by Seurat or by Klee, these novelties appear as fascinating sports or exceptions. By their very eccentricity these new means reinforce the formal strictness determining the dynasty of drawing in the West, which is more plastic, emphatic, violent, specialized and personal than the linear perfection of the almost anonymous calligraphy of the Orient.

Drawings are works of art of an intrinsic importance. They may be only, or also, preparations towards work in some other medium, but they are to be distinguished from working sketches. There is a real distinction between a drawing and a sketch. A drawing is a conscious design carried to a degree of finality. Certain drawings contain their achieved completeness as boldly as painted pictures. Antique drawings, and some contemporary ones hold their indisputable eminence in our artistic patrimony. Now, however, enhanced by a corruption of taste and by eager dealers, the prestige of a great hand is attached to any accidental scrap or scrawl it may have touched in passing. Sketches are reproduced, framed and sold as finished drawings and confound the critical sense. Drawings must be judged as responsible works of art, and sketches as working-plans towards other more developed stages. Or, at least those sketches which sometimes capture an impulse stronger than the completed picture of which they may have been the germ, are works of art of a different kind. Drawings have certain connections in the critical scale with prints, by their means and limitations, but they were not intended, primarily, for reproduction. Drawings are pushed to their particular notch of fulfillment and abandoned. Impulse or energy could do no more with that particular problem,

whose even partial fulfillment may nevertheless have resulted in a master-work; a step along a searching path is suddenly found to be a satisfactory goal; a research experiment turns out to be, in itself a great discovery.

Drawings, like any other objects of art, need working at. One must learn how to read them, like a poem, a painting, or more accurately, like a map. Drawings have to be studied, compared with other drawings, with other ways of drawing, so that one has cultivated or developed an appreciation in rendering line and form, comparable to a tutored taste in poetry or music. The rich literature of draughtsmanship is as full as the repertory of lyric verse or chamber-music. The question of comparative scale or grandeur does not obtain. A quartet, half-listened to, does not generate the immediate impression hammered out by a symphonic band. Fine drawings, half-looked at, or unlearnedly observed may first seem slight or pale. But some drawings contain a compact wealth of suggestion and independent interest exceeding apparent limits of size or modesty. A masterly line is so powerful that it resists exhaustion in being looked at. It can be explored indefinitely; it can be more fierce, sure or nervous in its passive strength than our muscular capacity for long regarding it. And, while a drawing can momentarily exhaust an eye, it also, and at the same time strengthens our nerves of vision and imagination. We can work on a drawing as at an athletic exercise.

Apart from fire, flood or other accidental disaster, paper lasts longer and drawings on it hold the first freshness of their author's intent clearer than almost any other media upon which artists must depend. Dry papyri, inked with almost unfaded brush-strokes are as fresh today, although separated by two thousand years as the Renaissance drawings at Windsor Castle, which in turn, are divided by nearly five hundred years from us, yet which seem as new now as if drawn an hour ago. Hard-coated or absorbent paper awaits an inked or lead or silver-point, the texture of its surface recalling its origin in shredded linen or pulped wood, rough or smooth, like cloth or ivory, the tint of the paper itself a bland field of white, rose or bistre, offering the pervasive couch of atmosphere for a swarm of lines and washes, whose coiled or pooling spontaneity, in spite of the lapse of centuries, has not been muted by the spoil of varnish or flaking pigment.

The initial touch of point to paper promises an entire design; like a germ, the first dot is the source of a whole new independent life or little world,—here on its plane surface, caught between four edges of a piece of paper. The first nuclear dot prolongs itself into a second and third, if one can imagine them as ever divided. The succession of dots, pushed or dragged, or literally, drawn across a page, constructs the line. Dots projected into a line instigate the description in the form of volumes and the volume in forms. The width of a line, its direction, contour, its spread or fineness, its dash or deliberation starts instantly to enclose a surface, or series of surfaces, which is the function of line to discover or uncover. Line cuts across a blank sheet like a chisel slashing across the plain face of a smooth slab. We recognize Assyrian or Egyptian mural reliefs as drawings incised into stone. Their deliberate processional profiles in a single eloquent plane define their individual plasticity as much or more than the chiselled, rounded out and half-released forms, cut away from the inlaid cartouche of hard-bit edges, which give their silhouette such a profound relief.

Nature herself establishes many criteria of draughtsmanship. The breaking line of a wave off shore, the pats of beasts in snow, the nets of spider-webs or the bony branched veining on the

back of leaves have each their special clarity of imprint, smudge or scratch. The abrupt sharp tracery or running swell of a line is legible as footprints in sand or the trace of a wheel. A pen or a brush on a page unconsciously echoes the movement of waves, the progress of tracks, veins in crystal or the snail's slow smear. Every drawing constructed of lines and smudges can be considered as the chart of an area, to be read like Mercator's projection or a topographical survey, the contours indicated at set intervals, its arterial rivers, vague swamps and confined seas. The conventional topographical signs denoting a lake or a chain of mountains are no less intellectualized than the screen of lines which formulate a bulge or scoop of muscle clad with flesh on bone,— a living landscape of hills and valleys which is also the defined analysis of volumes composing an animal, vegetable or a mineral form.

"Drawing," wrote the great Swiss pastellist, Liotard, "must be traced clean without being dry; firm without being hard or rigid; fluid without being soft; delicate and accurate without being mannered." The quality in a drawn line is so immediately apparent that it can be almost assessed or graded as if by its own metabolism. Its nervousness or placidity, its looseness or tightness, its brutality or grace is so insistent that one might even imagine a machine, tempered to such sensitivity that it could somehow transform the soul of a line into sound, in the way light is transferred electronically through space, so we might learn to listen to the imponderable melody of an outline, and gauge, by degrees, the sonority of a draughtsman's hand.

Baudelaire, contrasting the two great styles of draughtsmanship as exemplified in Ingres and Delacroix, felt perhaps, that he was making a distinction between the classicist and the romantic, but he added that such differences merge on the level of genius. "There are several kinds of drawings just as there are several colors—exact or stupid, physiognomical and imaginative. The first is negative, incorrect, by its very realism, faithful but absurd; the second is naturalistic, yet idealized, the drawing of a genius who knows how to select, arrange, correct, divine, subdue nature; the third finally, which is the noblest and strangest, may neglect nature yet represent another nature, corresponding to the mind and temperament of the author."

A hard line lies sharply on its surface. Lines on a wet field shatter or dissolve. A smudge is a violent, more summary dissolution of a line or a system of hatching which can be controlled and made suggestively useful to summon form by blur or blot. Hatchings have their neat, classic allocation of predetermined design, but the wash or smear when masterfully applied, can provide the apparently accidental relaxation and rightness of a lucky throw, which is here, then, skill rather than chance, but which permits a looser formulation, as opposed to logical order in a dryer system of shading by parallel or eccentric lines.

A line, protracted and projected, maps the frontiers of volumes, while interior areas indicating plastic forms, are italicized by bumps or bosses, depressions and protuberances netted in a skein of lines, hatched, brushed or dotted. Hatching, in its most disciplined and subtle organization always recalls its origin in the incised graver's lines of goldsmiths' work. Hatching defines only emphatic portions of forms chosen to represent a whole. Plasticity, roundness or relief is underlined or heightened in the development of systems of hatching,—each hatched part, to avoid an over-all monotony, applying only to the single evocative segment of shading or reflected light. These nets of hatching might be imagined as suggesting parts of

the surface of a suddenly illuminated, invisible but ever present coil of circles, black with crossed lines; a globe of linear tracery from which insistent or significant elements have been extracted or isolated, to define by rhythmic repetition, contrast or alternation, the desired roundness which alone can free a drawn form into its own air.

All hatchings and profiles are made of lines, single or crossed. All lines tend toward the circular, or to segments of a circle, no matter how flat or eccentric their ellipse, and poetically echo the bent horizon's continuous imperceptible curve. The life of a delineated line springs from the vitality of its curvature. The refinement and expressiveness in cross-hatching is in the whipped allocation of families of crossed curves. The lines composing a drawing, the outlines describing or defining form, or the hatching which intensifies the plasticity of volumes, each have the same function in their partial or suggestible relief, and tend, by their juxtaposition or contrast with areas left quite blank, to create an illusion of a completer roundness, or rather a complete sense of the round. "A true drawing is nothing but the shadow of a relief," wrote Cellini. "Thus, relief turns out to be the father of all drawing."

Little is flat in the natural world except surfaces man planes down or walls he builds up. By the turn of a wrist or the flick of a pen, a flat surface seems broken, and hence destroyed. A blot spreads into a butterfly's wing, or seen otherwise, with the light read as dark, we can see in it a man praying, a girl dancing, the back of a chair or an archipelago. Ristoro d'Arezzo wrote of the spots on the moon which many see as a human face, although "One sees in them a man on the gallows, another, two men tearing each other's hair out . . . others claim to see Cain and Abel . . . and there are some who see a bull or a horse." We know from contemporary research attending the Rorschach tests how precisely ambiguous spills and smears can be. There is also that ambiguous precision intensified by intellectual passion and manual dexterity, which is so baffling, and yet so impressive in many of the finest pen, brush and ink drawings. It is not so much that the artist fumbles towards his final vision, searching, pawing, hacking towards a rightness that will ring like a bell when it is finally reached. Rather, all overlapping contours suggest so much; the genuine form quivers beneath so many layers of possibility, wrapped in an halation of multiple choice, through which his outline must penetrate, and upon which he must impose his ultimate and irrevocable decision. Some drawings seem immediately surer than others. By the nature of its dryness, a pencil or silver-point lends itself to a firmer if fainter perfection of simple purpose, than the more reckless and fluid pen or brush. But the crystalline perfection in silver-point is paid for by its extreme demands of absolute skill. A half realized profile in the wiry line betrays weakness quicker than in other drawings. It is almost impossible to imagine a sketch in silver-point; silver-points are by their nature, drawings.

As soon as a dot feels the paper, there is created an ambivalence apparent on its surface. Does the dot rest upon it, like an impalpable spot? Does it pierce the surface like a burn or tear? Or does it emerge from the surface like a crumb? The initial dot, extended into a line, and the line into cutting or connecting boundaries between forms, pierced or raised, invents and supports its own lights and shadows. Variety in the monochromatic values of wash or hatching, and the quality of a line, wet or dry from pen or pencil, create their own gamut of color, pale or luminous, warm or cold. Elimination of a chromatic scale, the absence of a flexible palette, the focus on form rendered in the elastic atmosphere of a single tone, has never lim-

ited the intensity of a drawn picture. Sometimes, by accentuating linear, or purely plastic elements, the eye may even be more satisfied by its complete grasp of indicated structure than it otherwise might have been with a full richness of color. Van Gogh wrote, "In order to draw well, one ought to convey color through one's drawing."

In a drawing, which, if completely realized, lies somewhere between the more grandiose scales of sculpture and painting, between monochromatic form in the round whose only hue is its intense plasticity released in air, and luxuriant color whose plasticity arises from a release and harmony of tonal values on a plane surface, the eye can settle upon and devour the absorbing qualities of absolute line. This absoluteness, like an unaccompanied string or reed melody, is uniquely clear in the unerring chiselled, slightly metallic deposit of a silver-point, which cuts onto a paper's prepared surface and lies in it, after oxydization, like a hair wire of changeable gilt.

Line, flowing in a stream of consecutive points from the nerves of an artist's finger-tips, conducts its own almost somnambulistic energy, dreamlike in its undeterred automatism, but by no means hypnotized. Just as every dream is relevant if rightly read, since its loose fragments refer to some waking experience, so the spontaneous draughtsman's rapid line is supported by intuition based on past observation. The more complete the information or persistent the artist's practice, the more incandescent and conclusive his finished handiwork. This automatism is governed and guaranteed by a repetition of studies, a framework of factual knowledge slowly gained by close and loving familiarity,—by dissection, by analysis, by increasing sensitivity of touch and penetration in observation, and by main patience. The process mounts up to a complete assimilation of descriptive factors which can summarize a subject combining a multiplicity of shapes and aspects into one single moment, yet so completely that a single profile can dictate the three dimensions for a drawing to survive in its synthesis of a fourth,—as a liberated composition in space enduring indefinitely in time. "Is it not one of the characteristics of drawing," writes John Rewald, "that they are not immobile, that they breathe under the onlooker's eye? The signs assembled on paper are ready to come to life whenever we glance at them, to execute their rhythmic rondo, to sway hither and thither, to glide along on the whiteness of the sheet, carrying us away in the path of their silent interplay."

With such practice, by elimination of improvisation, by control of accident and caprice, and by the acceptance of a discipline of manual responsibility, which often even must conquer manual facility or superficial dexterity itself, any imagined concept of an artist is capable of legible achievement through the intense connection between his active mind and the muscles of hand and fingers in an almost blindly automatic relationship. The alacrity of mind and hand, the simultaneity of sensory perception transmitted instantaneously, Leonardo called *prestezza*, a sparking of physical, intellectual and moral energy which we also label gift, talent, or to a greater degree, genius. It is also, for most men, magic,—*prestezza*, prestidigitation, the employ of nimble fingers, the quickness of the hand that literally deceives the eye.

But however apparently thoughtless, the priceless initial instinctive gift, talent or genius is nourished by habitual but considered practice towards laconic precision. Precision is the enemy or absence of waste, the anonymous inscription which resists correction or corruption in the solvent processes of taste and time. Good drawing is also the victory of manual, motor

9

and moral necessity; good draughtsmanship declares what is firmly necessary for the realization of the dictating image, and little more. The intensity in an artist's revelation determines the conviction of his cursive or broken penmanship, handled in his idiosyncratic method, as individual as finger-print or hand-writing. There is his use of traditional styles, but without an insistent, personal manner. Mannerism is the imitation of models, of formulae of rendering at second-hand. Mannerism always tends towards the decorative. It attempts to approximate great past individual styles, which were themselves only established by the first-hand observation of nature. Mannerism is doomed at best to be a fashionable homage, at its worst a weak parody. In the most princely drawings, line is rendered impersonally, without manner, directly, as if we, spectator or critic, were viewing the sight independent of the seer, yet through his eyes and by his hand, fixed on visions inside his private crystal ball, full of shifting mirage, which an artist arrests at any crucial stage, when imagination, fed on its constant diet of natural discovery and strict observation, fairly bursts into poetic notion. Launched by the inspiriting image, caught in the seizure of its own self-induced crisis, the hand acts almost independently of the brain, propelling itself, as if commanded, or at least determined by the very line it delineates, drawn along, as it were, by the very process of drawing. One can define or rationalize the process only after a full recognition of what a line, or a complex of lines will then be seen to have described.

This line, or these lines, in the splendid drawings are never merely pattern. Lines do not exist, except in utilitarian art, only to propose decorations. Good draughtsmanship is not decorative. A good drawing, however well-designed, fluent, neat or bold is neither an exercise in calligraphy nor the filling of space with arabesques. If the draughtsman's line is considered as an electric needle, a thin hose of diamond dust, a tiny power-drill or a surgeon's microscopic knife, it is a continuous descriptive tool with a molten point, annotating the compulsive discovery or illumination of new forms. Watching the damp wall whose lime-soaked incrustations fused and flowed in the half-light, Leonardo found his famous griffons and mountain crags. "You may also see in them fights, strange figures and lively gestures, a quick play of human expression, odd apparel and innumerable other forms, which you then can distill into separate and well-realized shapes; for the same happens with these stones and walls as with the peal of bells, in whose sound you may discover every word and name you can imagine."

One thing suggested another. Accident inspired its chart of incident. The casual lead to the specific; rocks are mountains and mountains sleeping giants. A string of dots is transformed into the high-lights on a string of pearls. Sound divorced from its sequence is only noise, but sensitivity to its timbre and the measure of intervals between each note, previous silence and subsequent tones often conduct to melody. The pulse-like shift of sights and sounds in poetry, music and painting is the permanent kaleidoscope in an artist's eye. The intensity and scope of his exterior corroboration with his interior vision, by his craft; the frame of the moment of halt in his spectacular continuum, determines his degree of talent. Forms in the mind are endlessly reborn to be ceaselessly selected, like a swinging pendulum or a beating heart. Individual gifts guide us through these liquid landscapes and floating sounds.

Biographical Notes

Biographical Notes

1898-1917	Pavel Tchelitchew born, Moscow, Russia, September 21, of an aristocrat family. Educated by private tutors, and early influenced by the illustrations of Gustave Doré and the paintings of Vrubl.
1918-1920	With family, fled Bolshevik Revolution. Arrived Kiev, Fall, 1918. Attended drawing-classes, Kiev Academy. Encouraged by the constructivist scenic-designer, Alexandra Exter. Private instruction in painting by the Cubists, Tchacriguin and Rabinovitch. Worked in theatres, on poster-design, and as apprentice to local abstract painters.
1920-1921	Travelled in the Levant,—Constantinople, Sofia, etc.
1921-1923	Berlin. Theatre design for ballet and opera.
1923-1924	Paris. Reaction against Cubist and abstract painting. Portraits and landscapes.
1925	Exposed "Basket of Strawberries," Salon d'Automne. Friendship with Gertrude Stein.
1926	Showed with 'Neo-Romantic' group (Bérard, Berman, Leonide, Kristians Tonny) at the Galérie Druet. First multiple-images ("The Ship").
1927	Early circus pictures. South of France, North Africa, Algiers. Coffee-ground, sand and gouache mixed technique. 'Laconic' compositions.
1928-1929	Ballet, *Ode* (Nicolas Nabokoff-Leonide Massine) for Serge Diaghilew. Violent distortions in perspective and 'metamorphic' compositions. One-man shows in Paris and London.
1930-1931	Palette changes from monochromatic blues to monochromatic wine-reds. Series of paintings of Spahis and theatre-balconies.
1932-1933	Figures with metamorphic tattooing. Higher keyed palette. Ballet, *Errante* (Schubert-Koechlin-Balanchine), for Ballets 1933.
1934	Spain. Series of tennis-players and children. Use of 'characteristic perspective.' Arrived New York City, October. First American one-man show, Julien Levy Gallery.
1935	Italy. Ground-work for large painting "Phenomena." Series of freaks.
1936	Ballet, *Magic* (Mozart-Balanchine) and decorations for Paper Ball, Avery Memorial, Hartford, Connecticut.
1937-1938	"Phenomena" completed, Spring 1938. Portaits and silver-points. Ballet, *Nobilissima Visione* (St. Francis) (Hindemith-Massine), London.
1939-1940	Designed *Ondine*, play by Jean Giraudoux for Louis Jouvet, Paris. Weston, Connecticut. 'Autumn' palette; leaf-children and leaf drawings.
1940-1942	Summers, Derby Hill, Vermont. Metamorphic landscapes. Completed "Hide and Seek" (*Cache-Cache*), begun Summer 1940. One-man show, Museum of Modern Art. Ballets: *Concerto* (Mozart-Balanchine) and *Apollon Musagète* for Teatro Colon, Buenos Aires.
1943-1947	'Interior landscapes.' Work on large canvas "Paradise." Anatomical research and 'metamorphic' paintings investigating the human organism. One-man show, Durlacher Bros., New York City, January 1945.

11

Catalogue

Catalogue

James Thrall Soby : Catalogue of Tchelitchew Exhibition, Museum of Modern Art, New York, 1942. References to this Catalogue will be noted as Soby. In it, there is an extensive bibliography. References which have appeared since will be noticed in the Catalogue, as they occur. All dimensions are given in inches.

1 NIGHT AND DAY

Black india ink, pen and brush on white paper; 11¼ x 15.

Unsigned, undated.

Drawn, 1926, in the artist's studio, 150 Boulevard Montparnasse, Paris.

Collection: Durlacher Bros., New York City.

"In the fall of 1925 Tchelitchew had attempted his own solution of a problem which had engrossed abstract painters of the older generation, particularly Picasso, and which has supplied one of the most persistent themes in 20th century painting; the simultaneous presentation of several different aspects of the human head and figure." Soby: 1942.

2 THE MASK

Black india ink, pen and brush on white paper; 8¾ x 11¾.

Signed: P. Tchelitchew 1926.

Collection: Durlacher Bros., New York City.

Reproduced: *Tchelitchew*: Soby, p. 16.

Drawn, 1926, in the artist's studio, 150 Boulevard Montparnasse, Paris.

"Early in 1926 Tchelitchew extended his experiments with simultaneity to include the human figure as well as the head. Possibly the first step in this direction is represented by drawings of that year in which the figure is handled as a single image while two aspects of the head are suggested by the ingenious expedient of showing the subject in the act of peeling off a mask." Soby: 1942. A similar

'laconic' drawing (1925) is in the collection of James Johnson Sweeney Esq., New York City.

3 HARVESTERS

Black india ink, pen and brush on white paper; 11¼ x 17¼.

Unsigned, undated.

Collection: Monroe Wheeler Esq., New York City.

Reproduced: Soby, p. 45.

Drawn, Summer 1928, at the artist's country house, Guermantes, Seine-et-Marne, France. A gouache study of the same subject is in the collection of Mr. and Mrs. R. Kirk Askew, Jr., New York City. An oil painting of the same subject was, before World War II, in the collection of M. Pierre Loeb, Paris, for which a friend of the artist, Natasha Glasko, posed. (Reproduced, Soby, p. 45.)

4 CIRCUS FAMILY

Black india ink and brush on white paper; 11⅛ x 7¹¹⁄₁₆.

Signed: P. Tchelitchew, Paris 1929.

Collection: Mr. and Mrs. Morris Fish, New York City.

Drawn, 1929, at the artist's studio, 150 Boulevard Montparnasse, Paris, from memory after many visits to the four or five permanent Parisian one-ring circuses. An oil painting, in Burgundy reds, derived from the figure of the reclining clown at the top of the page is in the collection of M. Jean Stern, Lausanne, Switzerland. A gouache, "Clown Resting," showing the figure composed, as in Tchelitchew's other *portraits natures-mortes*, of pans, bottles, jugs and other familiar ob-

jects, is in the collection of George Gallowhur Esq., New York City. A related drawing is in the collection of Joseph Pulitzer Esq., St. Louis, Missouri. Both are reproduced, Soby, p. 48.

5 CIRCUS CHARACTERS

Black lead-pencil on white paper; 10½ x 17⅜.

Signed: P. Tchelitchew 1929.

Collection: Durlacher Bros., New York City.

Drawn, 1929, at the artist's studio, 150 Boulevard Montparnasse. One of a large number of studies drawn from memory. Miss Allanah Harper has an oil of fighting horses in England. The artist has a gouache of the same subject. "The Fallen Rider" (1930), an oil, formerly in the collection of Bernard Davis Esq., Philadelphia, is now in the collection of the Museum of Modern Art, New York City.

6 SEATED MAN

Black india ink, pen and brush on white paper; 10¾ x 17¾.

Signed: P. Tchelitchew 1928.

Collection: Durlacher Bros., New York City.

Drawn, Spring 1928, at the artist's studio, 150 Boulevard Montparnasse, Paris, as a study for a portrait of M. Jacques Stettiner, a friend. This is an outgrowth of the earlier 'laconic' compositions and an interest in the circus. (See Notes on Nos. 1, 2 and 5.)

7 STUDY FOR "THE BLUE CLOWN"

Black india ink, pen and brush on white paper; 10½ x 16.

Signed: P. Tchelitchew '29.

Collection: Museum of Modern Art, New York City (Mrs. Simon Guggenheim Fund).

Reproduced: Soby, p. 46.

Graham Reynolds: "Twentieth Century Drawings": London 1946, pl. 40. (Reference: pages 29-30.)

Exhibited: N. Y., Julien Levy, "A Decade of Painting: 1929-1939."
N. Y., Julien Levy, "Metamorphoses" by Pavel Tchelitchew, April 1942.
N. Y., Museum of Modern Art, "Tchelitchew," 1942, no. 89.
(N. Y., Museum of Modern Art, "New Acquisitions," 1942-1943.)
N. Y., Museum of Modern Art, "Modern Drawings," 1944.

Drawn, April 1929, at the artist's studio, 150 Boulevard Montparnasse, Paris. This drawing, prominent in a series of circus subjects, is a preliminary study for the oil in the collection of James Thrall Soby, Farmington, Connecticut. Other related drawings and paintings are owned by Joseph Pulitzer Esq., St. Louis, Missouri; Mr. and Mrs. Sherman Kent, Washington, D. C. and Durlacher Bros., New York City. (Reproduced, Soby, pages 46-47.) On the reverse of this drawing there are pencil sketches of the circus; four performers and a bicycle.

In May 1945, Tchelitchew commented on this drawing: "My interest of enlarging the time-moment by pulling together two unrelated aspects of the image—contrast of aspects—metamorphic genius. This is one of the earliest metamorphic drawings."

8 EDITH SITWELL

Sepia ink, pen and brush on bistre paper; 5½ x 8.

Signed: P. Tchelitchew '29.

Collection: James Gilvarry Jr. Esq. Brooklyn, N. Y.

Drawn, 1929, at the artist's new studio, 2 Rue Jacques Mawas, Paris XV. Tchelitchew met Edith Sitwell, the English poet and critic, in Paris in 1927. They were introduced by Gertrude Stein. He subsequently painted several portraits of her. This drawing is for an oil, 1930, at which time he also made a portrait head in wire and wax sculpture. He painted a large portrait in oils in 1937. (Reproduced: Soby, p. 70.) Tchelitchew drew cover-designs for two of Miss Sitwell's books, "The English Eccentrics" (London, 1931) and "Green Song," (New York, 1946).

9 GERTRUDE STEIN

Sepia ink, pen and brush on white paper; 10⅝ x 17⅝.

Signed: P. Tchelitchew 1931.

Collection: Edward Melcarth Esq., New York City.

Drawn, 1929, in the artist's studio, 2 Rue Jacques Mawas, Paris XV. Tchelitchew met Gertrude Stein in the Summer of 1925, through Miss Jane Heap, editor of "The Little Review," on the Pont Royale, just before the opening of the Salon d'Automne at the Tuilleries. To this exhibition Tchelitchew had sent his oil, "Basket of Strawberries" (Collection: Allen Porter, Esq., New York City), which marked a turning-point in his artistic career. He knew Miss Stein for several years. Another drawing of her is in the collection of Mrs. Charles B. Goodspeed, Chicago, Illinois. Tchelitchew is mentioned in "The Autobiography of Alice B. Toklas," pages 277-280.

10 SPAHI

Sepia ink, pen and brush on white paper; 10⁷⁄₁₆ x 8³⁄₁₆.

Signed: P. Tchelitchew '31.

Collection: John Yeon Esq., Portland, Oregon.

Drawn, 1929, in the artist's studio, 2 Rue Jacques Mawas, Paris XV. Tchelitchew had a friend in the French colonial North African regiment of Spahis, who gave him a uniform which inspired him to make a series of drawings and paintings of various models in the jacket, baggy trousers and fez. An oil painting of this subject is in the collection of James Thrall Soby Esq., Farmington, Connecticut. (Reproduced, Soby, p. 57.)

11 SEATED SPAHI

Sepia ink, pen and brush on bistre paper; 10¼ x 13¾.
Signed: P. Tchelitchew (Undated).

Collection: Mr. and Mrs. Russell Lynes, New York City.

Exhibited: Tchelitchew Exhibition, Museum of Modern Art, 1942 (Cat. no. 100).

Drawn, 1931, in the artist's studio, 2 Rue Jacques Mawas, Paris XV. An oil of the same subject is in the collection of Madame Alexandra Zasouailoff, Paris, and a pastel is at Durlacher Bros., New York City.

12 THE CONCERT

Black india ink and pen on white paper; 10⁷⁄₁₆ x 8³⁄₁₆.

Signed: P. Tchelitchew '32.

Collection: Van Truex Esq., New York City.

Drawn, 1932, at the artist's studio, 2 Rue Jacques Mawas, Paris XV. This is one of a series of some fifty drawings of similar subjects, which are related to the oil *Le Concert* (Collection: Edward James Esq., London). However, none of the drawings actually indicate the final composition, which is reproduced, Soby, p. 64.

13 THE LOVERS

Sepia ink, pen and brush on bistre paper; 8 x 10½.

Unsigned, undated.

Collection: Madame Paul Kochanski, New York City.

Drawn, Winter 1931, at the artist's studio, 2 Rue Jacques Mawas, Paris XV. This drawing of an imaginary subject had no models and was not a study for any subsequent painting.

14 ORPHEUS

Sepia ink, pen and brush on white paper; 17⁷⁄₁₆ x 22.

Signed: P. Tchelitchew '31.

Collection: Durlacher Bros., New York City.

Drawn, Spring 1931, at the artist's studio, 2 Rue Jacques Mawas, Paris XV. One of a series of *portraits natures-mortes*. The construction in the background, which appears also in numerous studies for *La Dame au Cirque* (1931; Collection: James Thrall Soby Esq., Farmington, Connecticut) was inspired by the demolition of a cinema theatre of the

epoch of 1900, on the Rue de la Convention, near the artist's new studio. The legend of Orpheus had interested Tchelitchew for many years. In 1937, he designed the scenery and costumes for a danced production of Gluck's *Orfeo*, choreography by George Balanchine, for the American Ballet at the Metropolitan Opera House, New York City.

15 THE MARNE

Sepia ink, pen and brush on white paper; $14\frac{1}{2}$ x $10\frac{1}{2}$.

Signed: P. Tchelitchew '32.

Collection: Durlacher Bros., New York City.

Drawn, Summer 1932, at Guermantes, Seine-et-Marne, France. Tchelitchew made many drawings of threatening cloud-figures at this time, moved by the general fear of European war. He had intended them as studies for a large picture which he never commenced. As he said: "Events painted the canvas a little later." However, certain elements from this series, notably the bathers, reappear in several large gouaches, notably in one now in the collection of Henry McIlhenny Esq., Germantown, Pennsylvania. A decisive battle of the first World War was fought September, 1914 on the banks of the river Marne.

16 THE HANDS OF APOLLO

Sepia ink, pen and brush on white paper; $10\frac{15}{16}$ x $17\frac{1}{2}$.

Unsigned and undated.

Collection: Durlacher Bros., New York City.

Drawn, 1931, at the artist's studio, 2 Rue Jacques Mawas, Paris XV. This drawing is related to a series of portraits composed from elements of still-life *(portraits natures-mortes)* in which various objects such as fruit, kitchen utensils, nets and plaster casts are arranged to suggest heroic or fantastic human personages. (See Nos. 9, 14 and 17.)

In 1942, Tchelitchew designed the ballet *Apollon Musagète* (Apollo, Leader of the Muses), music by Igor Strawinsky, choreography by George Balanchine, for the Teatro Colon, Buenos Aires, Argentina. The designs are now in the Department of Theatre Design, Museum of Modern Art, New York City. The costume and head-dress of Apollo recalls the plaster head in this drawing. (Reproduced, *Dance Index,* Tchelitchew issue, Vol. III, nos. 1 and 2, January-February, 1944, pages 2 and 31.)

17 LA DAME AU CIRQUE

Sepia ink, pen and brush on white paper; $12\frac{1}{16}$ x $17\frac{1}{4}$.

Signed: P. Tchelitchew '30.

Collection: Oliver B. Jennings Esq., New York City.

Drawn, 1931, at the artist's studio, 2 Rue Jacques Mawas, Paris XV. This composition follows, in general ideas, the results of the portrait of Jacques Stettiner (No. 6). The woman is conceived as Queen of the Arena, the centre of the Ring, and herself a circus, the centre of a world which is herself. The architectural construction derives from the demolition of an old cinema, also seen in "Orpheus" (No. 14). This is one of a series of drawings terminating in an oil painting of the same name, now in the possession of James Thrall Soby Esq., Farmington, Connecticut. (Reproduced, Soby, p. 54.)

18 BOY WITH NASTURTIUMS

Sepia ink, pen and brush on white paper; $10\frac{5}{8}$ x $14\frac{1}{2}$.

Signed: P. Tchelitchew 1931.

Collection: Madame Maria Hugo, New York City.

Exhibited: Tchelitchew Exhibition, Museum of Modern Art, 1942 (Cat. no. 103).

Drawn, Summer 1931, at Guermantes, Seine-et-Marne, France. The artist had a garden with all sort of flowers and vegetables which he drew and painted.

19 THE FLOWERED CLOUD

Sepia ink, pen and brush on white paper; $8\frac{15}{16}$ x $12\frac{3}{16}$.

Signed: P. Tchelitchew '32.

Collection: Durlacher Bros., New York City.

Drawn, Summer 1932, at Guermantes, Seine-et-Marne, France. A similar drawing, "Boy With Anemones" is in the collection of Mr. and Mrs. R. Kirk Askew, New York City.

20 LA MUSIQUE

Sepia ink, pen and brush on white paper; 10¼ x 7⅞.

Signed: P. Tchelitchew '32.

Collection: The Wadsworth Athenaeum and Morgan Memorial, Hartford, Connecticut.

Exhibited: Tchelitchew Exhibition, Museum of Modern Art, 1942 (Cat. no. 115).

Reproduced: Soby, p. 88.

Drawn, 1932, at the artist's studio, 2 Rue Jacques Mawas, Paris XV. One of a series of studies towards the oil painting "The Chinese Song," in the collection of Edward James Esq., London. This drawing is related to the oil "Natalie Paley as Ophelia" (1932), now in the collection of Mr. and Mrs. John C. Wilson, New York City. (Reproduced, Soby, p. 55.)

21 AFRICA

Black india ink and pen on white paper; 8¼ x 10½.

Signed: P. Tchelitchew '32.

Collection: Durlacher Bros., New York City.

Exhibited: Tchelitchew Exhibition, Museum of Modern Art, 1942 (Cat. no. 114).

Drawn, 1932, at the artist's studio, 2 Rue Jacques Mawas, Paris XV. The artist drew a series of studies after reading the fantastic books of Raymond Roussel, particularly *Impressions d'Afrique, Nouvelles Impressions d'Afrique* and *Locus Solus*. The drawings were not intended as illustrations.

22 THE STAIR

Sepia ink, pen and brush on white paper; 7¾ x 11¾.

Signed: P. Tchelitchew '32.

Collection: Mrs. Huttleston Rogers, New York City.

Drawn, 1932, at the artist's studio, 2 Rue Jacques Mawas, Paris XV. This drawing, from imagination, is not unrelated to a reading of Dostoevski's "Crime and Punishment." At this time, the artist was struck repeatedly by a sense of the immanence and aftermath of violent events. The event itself was never thought to have been actually described. (See note on "The Marne," no. 15.)

23 LA RUE BLOMET

Black india ink, pen and brush on white paper; 11¾ x 7¾.

Signed: P. Tchelitchew '33.

Collection: Mrs. Huttleston Rogers, New York City.

Drawn, 1933, at the artist's studio, 2 Rue Jacques Mawas, Paris XV. The artist was struck by the apparent sordidness of this street, which crosses the Rue de la Convention, and through which he frequently passed from the home of his friend, Raul Levin, to his own studio. This drawing was done from memory, inspired by the sense of emptiness of a place, threatened or deserted by some violent event. (See notes on nos. 15 and 22.)

24 PETER THE GREAT

Sepia pen and ink on white paper; 9¾ x 12 11/16.

Signed: P. Tchelitchew '34.

Collection: Durlacher Bros., New York City.

Drawn, 1934, at the artist's studio, 2 Rue Jacques Mawas, Paris XV. The artist made a number of drawings of children seen in violent forced perspective, some with tennis-rackets, others with large ears, anticipating the key-figure of the Infant Prodigy in the Red Shirt, in his large canvas "Phenomena" (1936-1938). A pastel related to this drawing is in the collection of Edward James Esq., London. Other similar drawings are owned by *View* Magazine and Durlacher Bros., New York City.

25 **THE EAR**

Charcoal crayon on white paper; 12⅝ x 19¼.

Signed: P. Tchelitchew 1934 (signature and dedicatory inscription added, 1936).

Collection: Mrs. Alfred H. Barr, New York City.

Drawn, 1934, at the artist's studio, 2 Rue Jacques Mawas, Paris XV. This is one of a series of studies for the oil "The Tennis Player," now in the collection of Sir Kenneth Clark, London, which is reproduced, Soby, p. 64.

"After completing a small oil 'Dream of a Girl,' whose eerie *Turn of the Screw* romanticism pervaded many of the painter's studies of children, Tchelitchew began working on a major theme—'the tennis players.' He commenced two very large pastel heads of a baby tennis player . . . accompanied by numerous drawings, many of which were side views of the head of a girl with an enormously enlarged ear . . ." (Soby, p. 25 *et seq.*)

26 **ITALIAN FAMILY**

Silver-point on white prepared paper; 12 x 17.

Signed: P. Tchelitchew (undated).

Collection: Mr. and Mrs. Lincoln Kirstein, New York City.

Exhibited: Tchelitchew Exhibition, Museum of Modern Art, 1942 (Cat. no. 138).

Drawn, 1937, in New York City, from memories of Italy, as part of the early studies for the large canvas "Phenomena" (1936-1938). In this year, Tchelitchew made a great number of silver-point drawings, many of the finest of which are in the collection of Edward James Esq., London.

27 **CHARLES HENRI FORD**

Silver-point on white prepared paper; 13 x 19⅞.

Signed: P. Tchelitchew 1937, N. Y. C.

Collection: Miss Edith Wetmore, New York City.

Drawn, 1937, in New York City. Tchelitchew met Ford, a poet and editor of *View*, an advance-guard magazine, in Paris, 1931. *View* has frequently published reproductions of and articles about the artist's work. For May, 1942 *View* published an issue devoted to Tchelitchew. This drawing is related to a series of drawings for "Phenomena" (1936-1938). There are other portraits of the same subject, notably an oil. (Reproduced, Soby, p. 62.)

28 **THE RUSSIAN SINGER**

Red ink and pen on white paper; 16 x 12½.

Signed: P. Tchelitchew '35.

Collection: Mr. and Mrs. Lincoln Kirstein, New York City.

Exhibited: Tchelitchew Exhibition, Museum of Modern Art, 1942 (Cat. no. 127).

Drawn, Summer 1935, at Malcesine, Lago di Garda, Italy. One of a large series employing Tchelitchew's 'characteristic perspective,' or several vanishing-points within a single composition, to heighten a sense of precipitation, and to give to each figure the particular foreshortening most evocative or descriptive of its essential character. The figure of the Singer, may be found altered and amplified in the upper left of "Phenomena," the large canvas (1935-1938) now in the collection of the artist. (Reproduced, Soby, p. 75.)

29 **KING LEAR**

Blue ink and pen on white paper; 16¾ x 13⅞.

Signed: P. Tchelitchew '37.

Collection: Durlacher Bros., New York City.

Drawn, Summer 1937, at Ischia, near Naples, Italy. Tchelitchew had designed an entire production of John Webster's tragedy "The Duchess of Malfi" which was to have been produced by The Mercury Theatre, Orson Welles, director. The many gouache drawings for scenery and costumes are now in the collection of Mrs. Huttleston Rogers, New York City. They have never been reproduced. Tchelitchew also planned for Welles a "King Lear," to have been presented in conjunction

with Arthur Hopkins, and he made designs towards a "Tempest." None of the plays were realized. This drawing was done after a reading of the play; it is not an actual costume sketch.

30 DANCER

Red ink and white gouache on rose paper; 8¾ x 13½.

Signed: P. Tchelitchew 1937.

Collection: Mr. and Mrs. Lincoln Kirstein, New York City.

Exhibited: Tchelitchew Exhibition, Museum of Modern Art, 1942 (Cat. no. 139).

Drawn, New York City, early Spring 1937, as part of the study for "Phenomena," the large canvas (1935-1938), now in the collection of the artist.

31 THE HANDS OF KOPEIKINE

Red ink and pen on dark beige cardboard; 9⅜ x 15⅝.

Signed: P. Tchelitchew '37.

Collection: Durlacher Bros., New York City.

Drawn, early Spring 1937, at the artist's studio, 235 East 72nd Street, New York City. Tchelitchew met the Russian pianist Nicolas Kopeikine in New York upon his first arrival from Paris in 1934. Both Russians, they had a common interest in music and ballet, although they had not previously known each other. Kopeikine frequently served as pianist for George Balanchine with whom Tchelitchew collaborated on the ballets *Errante* (1933), *Magic* (1936), *Orpheus* (1936), *Balustrade* (1941), etc., etc.

32 NICOLAS KOPEIKINE

Silver-point on white prepared paper; 12¾ x 19.

Signed: P. Tchelitchew '37.

Collection: Dr. Paul J. Sachs, Cambridge, Massachusetts.

Drawn, early Spring 1937, at the artist's studio, 235 East 72nd Street, New York City. Similar silver-points of this subject are in the collection of Dr. Burrill B. Crohn and Edaldji Dinsha Esq., both of New York City. Tchelitchew also made a series of fantastic drawings of the pianist Kopeikine, dressed as a child prodigy, as Mozart's 'Queen of the Night,' and in various operatic disguises.

33 FREDERICK ASHTON

Silver-point on white prepared paper; 12⅛ x 18.

Signed: P. Tchelitchew 1938 London.

Collection: The Fogg Museum of Art, Harvard University, Cambridge, Massachusetts.

Exhibited: Tchelitchew Exhibition, Museum of Modern Art, 1942 (Cat. no. 146).

Drawn, May 1938, London. Tchelitchew had known Ashton, the English dancer and choreographer since 1929, when he was a member of the ballet company of Madame Ida Rubenstein. During the Summer of 1938 the painter was in Paris and London preparing the scenery and costumes for the ballet *Nobilissima Visione* (St. Francis) (Paul Hindemith-Léonide Massine), which was presented July 21, 1938 at Drury Lane by the Ballet Russe de Monte Carlo. (Designs for this ballet are in the Department of Theatre Design, Museum of Modern Art, New York City.) Ashton came to America in 1934 to arrange dances for the Virgil Thomson-Gertrude Stein opera "Four Saints in Three Acts." He is also known in the United States for his ballets *Devil's Holiday* (Scarlatti-Berman) and *Les Patineurs* (Meyerbeer-Beaton).

34 THE WINDOW

Pen and blue ink on white paper; 18 x 13¹⁵⁄₁₆.

Signed: P. Tchelitchew '37.

Collection: Durlacher Bros., New York City.

Drawn, June 1937, at Ischia, near Naples, Italy. One of a large series of drawings of characteristic Neapolitan heads framed by architecture; others are in the collections of Wright Ludington Esq., Santa Barbara, California and Mrs. Harry Dunham, New York City.

35 NEW YORK PERSPECTIVE

Sepia ink and pen on white paper; 16¾ x 13¾.

Signed: P. Tchelitchew '37.

Collection: Durlacher Bros., New York City.

Drawn, April 1937, at the artist's studio, 235 East 72nd Street. The view is from the tenth floor, facing north. In the upper right hand corner of the large canvas "Phenomena" (1936-1938), there are portions of a modern metropolis. This drawing, however, is purely an observation of nature.

36 MOTHER AND CHILD

Silver-point on white prepared paper; 16 x 12½.

Signed: P. Tchelitchew '38.

Collection: Durlacher Bros., New York City.

Drawn, May 1938, London. This is one of a series of drawings of the poor in Tchelitchew's 'characteristic perspective' (see note, no. 28), made as part of studies for figures in the lower left hand portion of the large canvas "Phenomena" ((1935-1938). However, it is not a study for any particular figure in it. Other related drawings are in the collection of Edward James Esq., London.

37 SLEEPING MOUNTAIN

Blue ink and pen on white paper; 17¼ x 10¾.

Signed: P. Tchelitchew 1939.

Collection: Durlacher Bros., New York City.

Exhibited: Tchelitchew Exhibition, Museum of Modern Art, 1942 (Cat. no. 157).

Drawn, June-July 1939, at Saint Jorioz, Lac d'Annecy, Haute Savoie, France. This drawing is related to the painting "Fata Morgana," in the collection of Edward James Esq., London, and to a series of metamorphic landscapes, which anticipate an extensive series of similar subjects done later at Derby Hill, Vermont. An oil, "The Lovers," of two

sleeping mountain-figures is in the collection of the artist, New York City.

38 THE BOAT

Bistre ink and brush on cream-colored paper; 10⅛ x 14⅜.

Signed: P. Tchelitchew '35.

Collection: Monroe Wheeler Esq., New York City.

Exhibited: Tchelitchew Exhibition, Museum of Modern Art, 1942 (Cat. no. 147).

Drawn, Summer 1935, at Malcesine, Lago di Garda, Italy, in one of a large series of children, freaks and anomalies of nature, preparatory to the painting of the large canvas "Phenomena" (1935-1938), now in the collection of the artist.

39 THE KISS

Black india ink and pen on white paper; 8$\frac{7}{16}$ x 10⅞.

Signed: P. Tchelitchew 1941.

Collection: Durlacher Bros., New York City.

Drawn, September 1941, at Derby Hill, Vermont, immediately preceding the series of metamorphic landscapes (nos. 40 and 41). Tchelitchew drew these studies after having heard poems of Baudelaire read aloud. They were not intended either as illustration, or as preparation for a picture, and are quite disassociated from drawings in the series that came before and after.

40 THE LION OF MICHAELANGELO

Black india ink, pen and wash on white paper; 8⅜ x 10⅞.

Signed: P. Tchelitchew '41.

Collection: The Museum of Modern Art, New York City (Gift of Miss Edith Wetmore).

Exhibited: N. Y., Julien Levy, "Metamorphoses" by Pavel Tchelitchew, April 1942.

N. Y., Museum of Modern Art, "Modern Drawings," 1944.

Museum of Modern Art Circulating Exhibition, European Artists in United States, 1945-1946.

Reproduced: "Modern Drawings," ed. by Monroe Wheeler, N. Y., Museum of Modern Art, 1944, p. 71.

Drawn, late September 1941, Derby Hill, Vermont, the next to last in a series in which a certain automatism and control of accidental suggestive elements play an important part. It was already cold in Vermont; the artist felt he could not paint, hence lavished considerable attention on these minute compositions. Others are in the collections of Mrs. Huttleston Rogers and Mr. and Mrs. Kirk Askew, New York City. Perhaps the finest, "American Eagle" in the Askew collection, is too large to reproduce in a reduction. Others are in the possession of Durlacher Bros., Wright Ludington Esq., Santa Barbara, and the Museum of Modern Art, New York City.

41 WINDOW AT THE END OF THE WORLD

Black india ink, pen and wash on white paper; 10¾ x 9¹¹⁄₁₆.

Signed: P. Tchelitchew '41.

Collection: Dr. and Mrs. Edgar Wind, Northampton, Massachusetts.

Drawn, late September 1941, Derby Hill, Vermont, the last of a series of metamorphic landscapes, which involved elements of automatism and organized accident in the flow of wash and control of profile.

42 ALEXANDER BULL

Lead pencil on white paper; 12½ x 16⅜.

Signed: P. Tchelitchew '41.

Collection: Harry Adsit Bull Esq., New York City.

Drawn, December 1941, New York City. Harry Bull, a friend of the artist, had been editor of the magazine *Town & Country* since 1934. For him, Tchelitchew had painted several covers. This drawing is inscribed "To my dear Harry a Baby Alexander's 9 month old portrait with best wishes for 1942 from Pavlik."

43 MADAME PAUL KOCHANSKI

Black india ink, pen and brush on white paper; 8½ x 10⅞.

Signed: P. Tchelitchew N.Y.C. '42.

Collection: Madame Paul Kochanski, New York City.

Drawn, Spring 1942, New York City. Madame Kochanski, wife of the Polish violin virtuoso and teacher, had been a friend of the painter since 1918, when they had met at the time of the Revolution in Kiev, Russia, and where he had painted her. This drawing bears a dedicatory inscription in Russian.

44 THE FLOWER OF SIGHT

Black india ink and brush on white paper; 14½ x 11⅜.

Signed: P. Tchelitchew '44.

Collection: Henry McIlhenny Esq., Germantown, Pennsylvania.

Exhibited: Tchelitchew Exhibition, Durlacher Bros., New York City, January 1945.

Drawn, January 1944, at the artist's studio, 360 East 55th Street, New York City. This is one of a large series of anatomical studies in consecutive categories of the painter's various periods,—the 'laconic' figures the *portraits natures-mortes,* the metamorphic landscapes—now, the 'interior landscapes.' Their basis is the transparent, or translucent rendering of the human body, or portions of it. Successively he has treated the head, the eye, the ear, the throat and the entire figure. While the anatomical basis has close reference to fact, the drawings are constantly transformed. The cover of the magazine *View* for December 1943 (Series III, No. 4) reproduces in color, a related gouache, now in the collection of Edward James Esq., Los Angeles. An article by Parker Tyler, "Human Anatomy as the Expanding Universe," *View,* Vol. 7, no. 3, May 1947 reproduces a number of Tchelitchew's most recent paintings in oil and gouache, for which the anatomical drawings here reproduced served as studies.

45 THE CRYSTAL GROTTO

Black india ink, pen and wash on white paper; 11 x 14.

Signed: P. Tchelitchew '44.

Collection: Museum of Modern Art, New York City.

Exhibited: Tchelitchew Exhibition, Durlacher Bros., New York City, January 1945.

Drawn, Spring 1943, at the artist's studio, 360 East 55th Street, New York City. Study for painting "The Crystal Grotto" (1943) in collection of Edward James Esq., Los Angeles. One of a series of 'interior landscapes.' Tchelitchew has made many drawings of the bony structure of the head. All of his anatomical research results in paintings of the human body as living mechanism and individual universe, and have little relation to ideas of mortality or physical corruption.

46 STUDY FOR "THE LADY OF SHALOTT"

Black india ink, pen and wash on white paper; 11 x 16.

Signed: P. Tchelitchew '44.

Collection: George Platt Lynes Esq., Los Angeles, California.

Exhibited: Tchelitchew Exhibition, Durlacher Bros., New York City, January 1945.

Drawn, Spring 1944, in the artist's studio, 360 East 55th Street, New York City. One of a series of 'interior landscapes.' The oil painting, for which this is a study, is now in the collection of Edward James Esq., Los Angeles. The lower right hand quarter of Tchelitchew's large allegory "Hide and Seek" (1940-1942) now in the Museum of Modern Art, New York City, contains in the transparent, crystal back of the figure of Winter, germs for the future anatomical research. George Lynes' collection also contains Tchelitchew's "Golden Leaf," a highly realized gouache painting of a human figure, the first independently achieved painting after "Hide and Seek."

47 ELEMENTAL HEAD

Black india ink, pen and brush on white paper; 11⅛ x 14.

Signed: P. Tchelitchew 1945.

Collection: Mr. and Mrs. Lincoln Kirstein, New York City.

Drawn, Summer 1945, Derby Hill, Vermont. One of a series of the artist's 'interior landscapes,' of which there are several large gouache and oil paintings.

48 THE TRIBUTARIES

Grey wash and brush, red pen and ink on white paper, 11⅛ x 14.

Signed: P. Tchelitchew '45.

Collection: Edward James Esq., Los Angeles, California.

Drawn, Summer 1945, at Derby Hill, Vermont. One of a series of the artist's 'interior landscapes.' The arteries are indicated in red ink. In 1941, Tchelitchew had drawn a series of costume sketches for a projected ballet *The Cave of Sleep* (Paul Hindemith-George Balanchine) which was not produced. The drawings are now in the Department of Theatre Design, Museum of Modern Art, New York City. Tchelitchew conceived a series of ballet *entrées*, of dancers whose costumes had elements from the muscular, nervous, lymphatic and arterial systems.

Plates

3

To Doris and Morris
with my friendly
always, Pavlik

P. Tchelitchew
Paris 1929

4

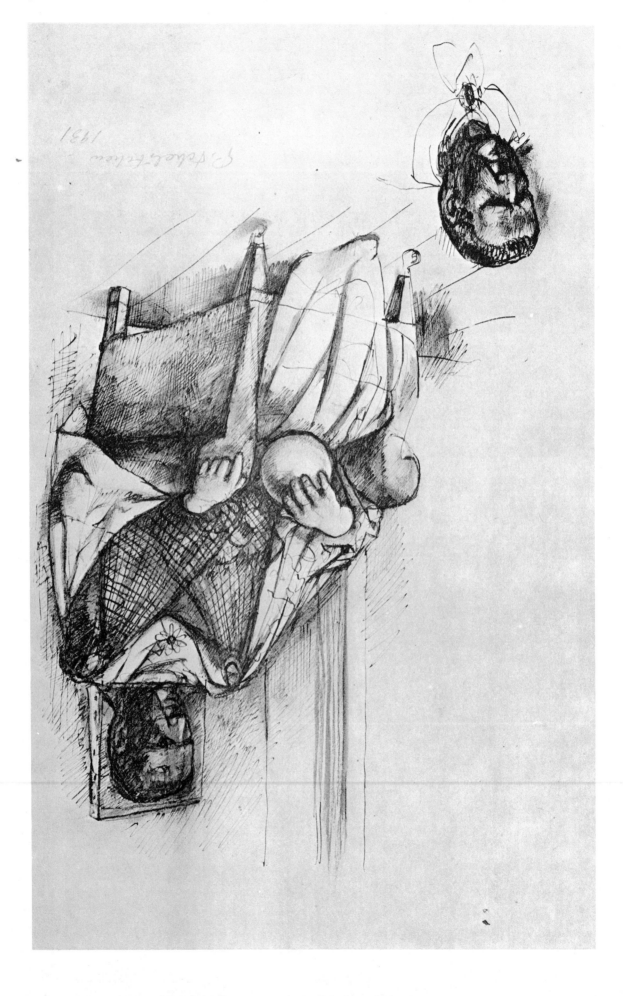

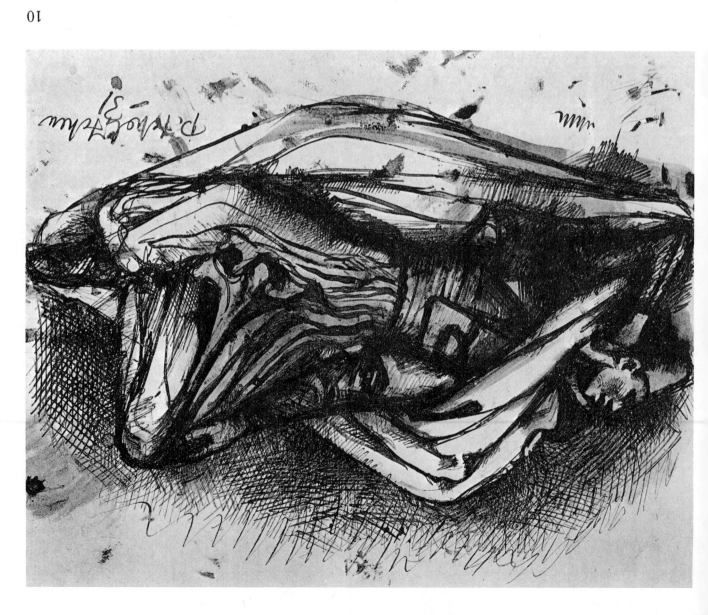

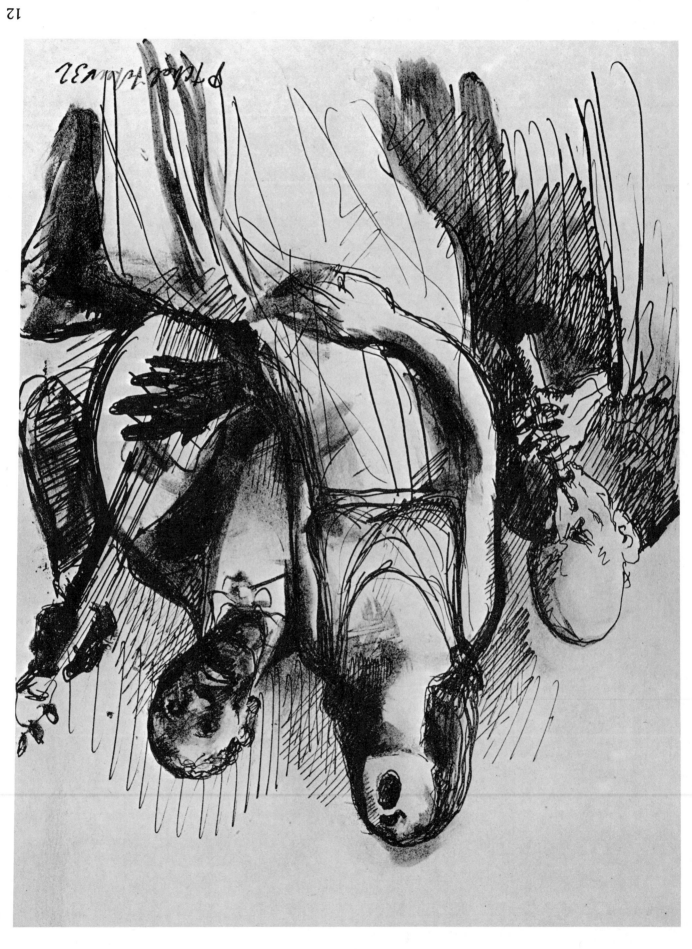

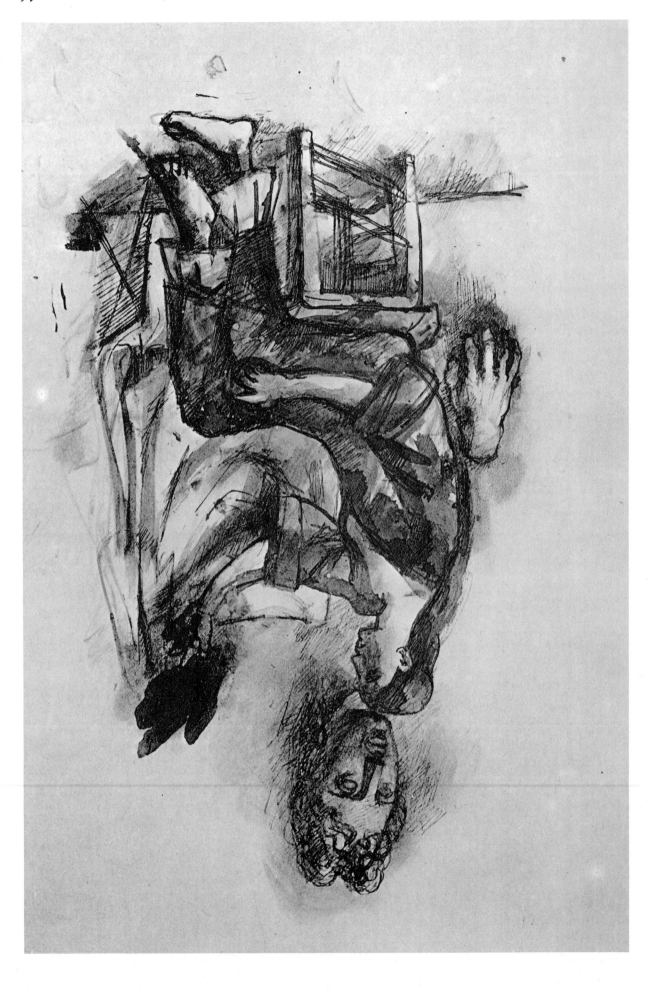

Belonging to Maria Hugo.

P. Tchelitchew
1931

18

20

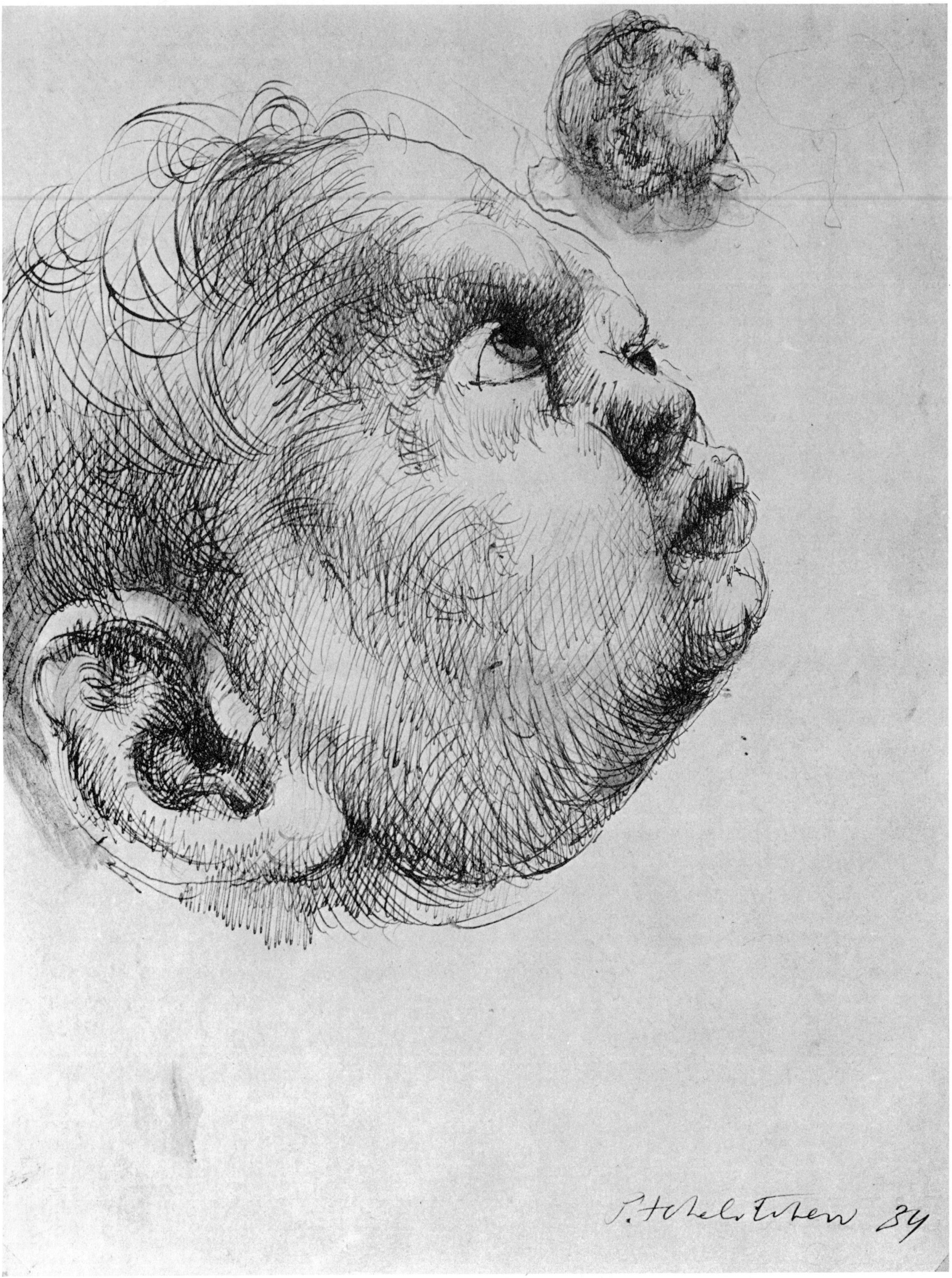

24

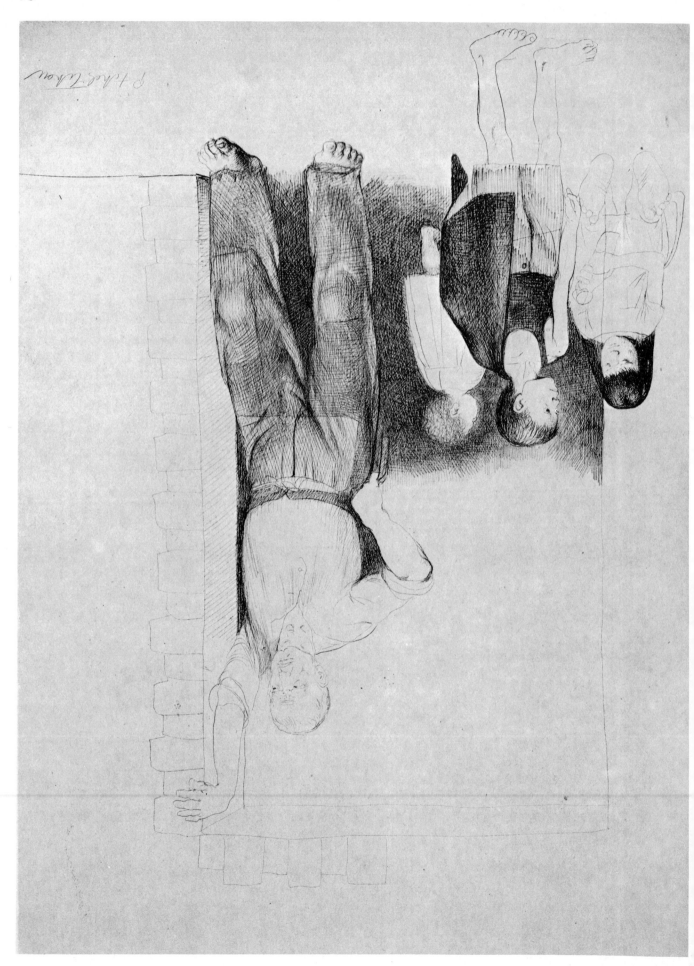

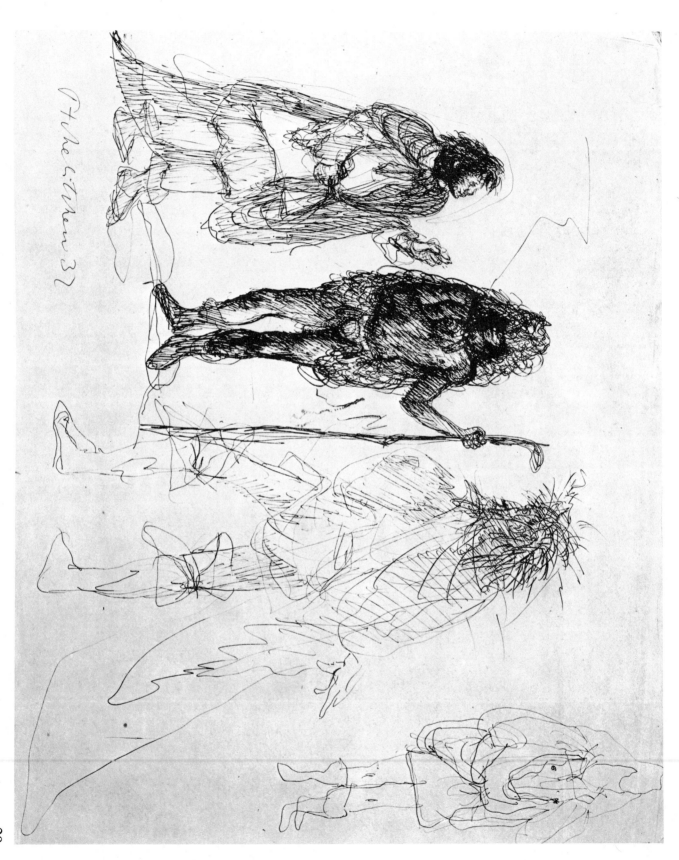

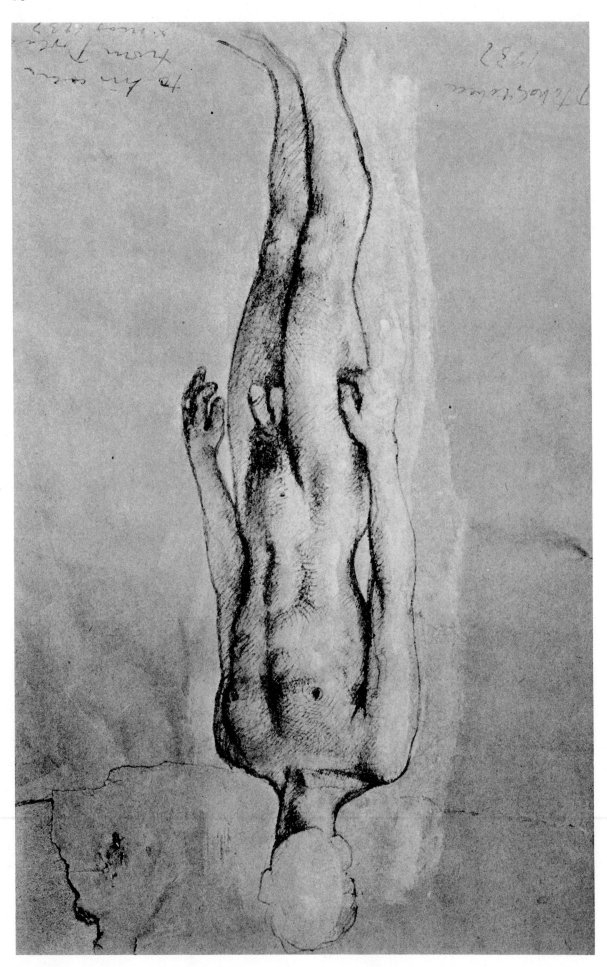

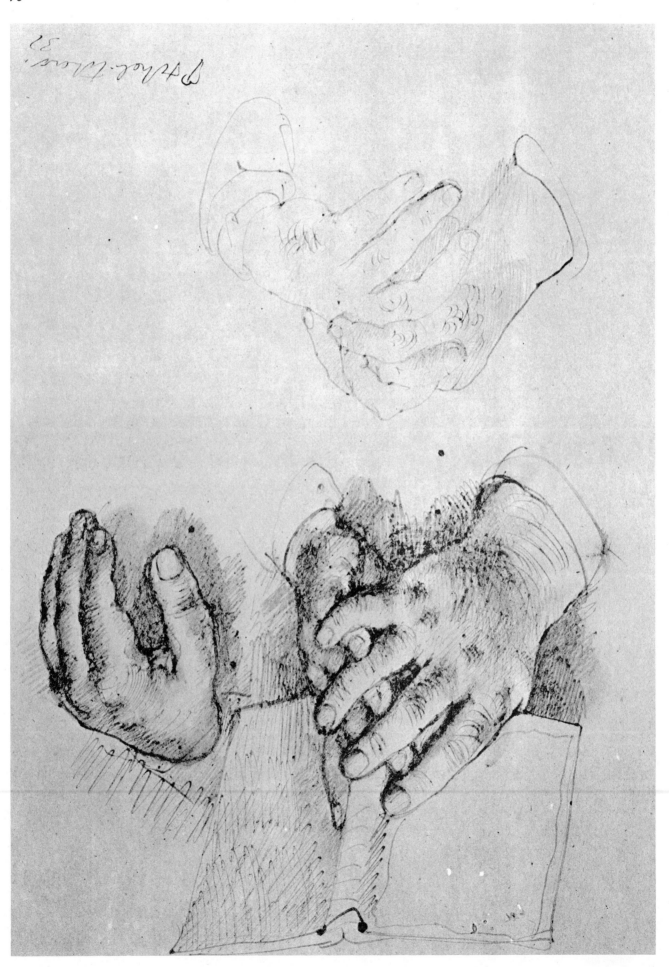

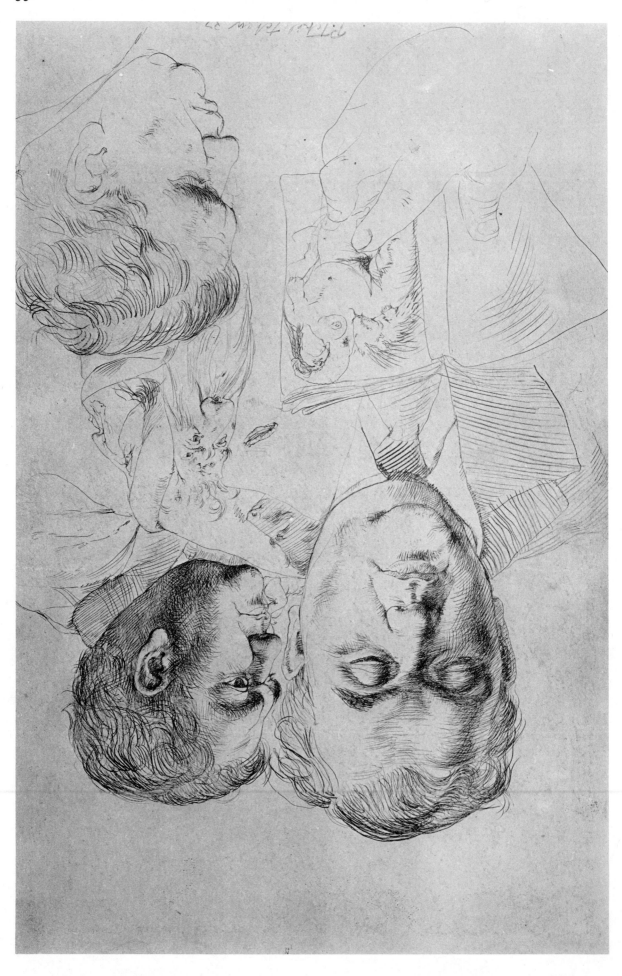

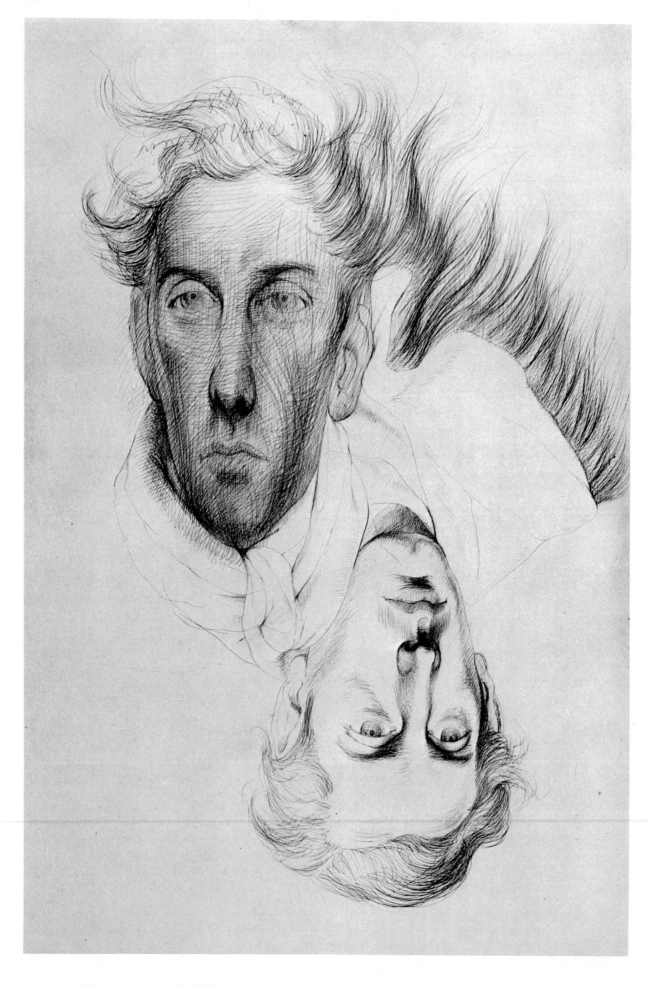

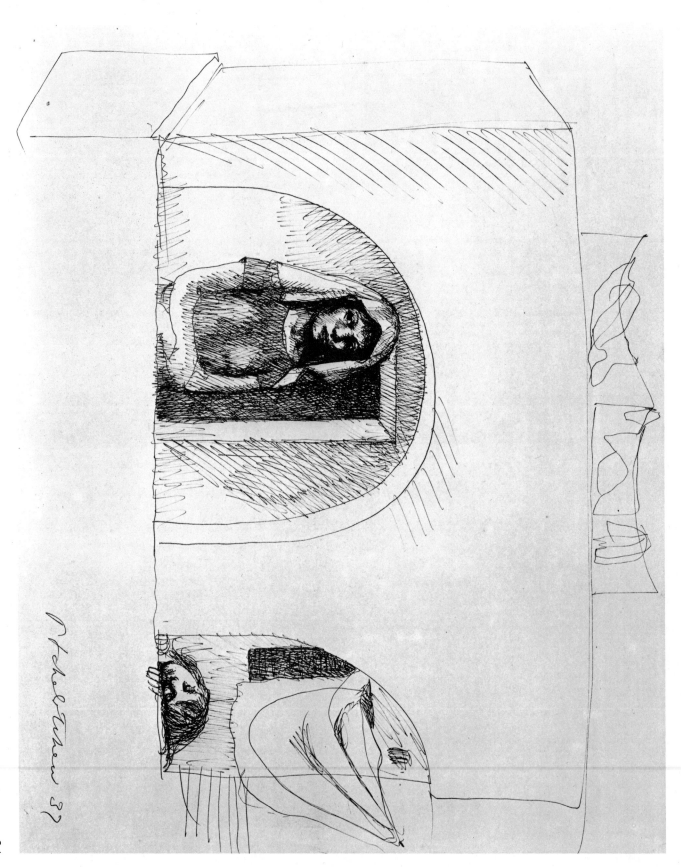

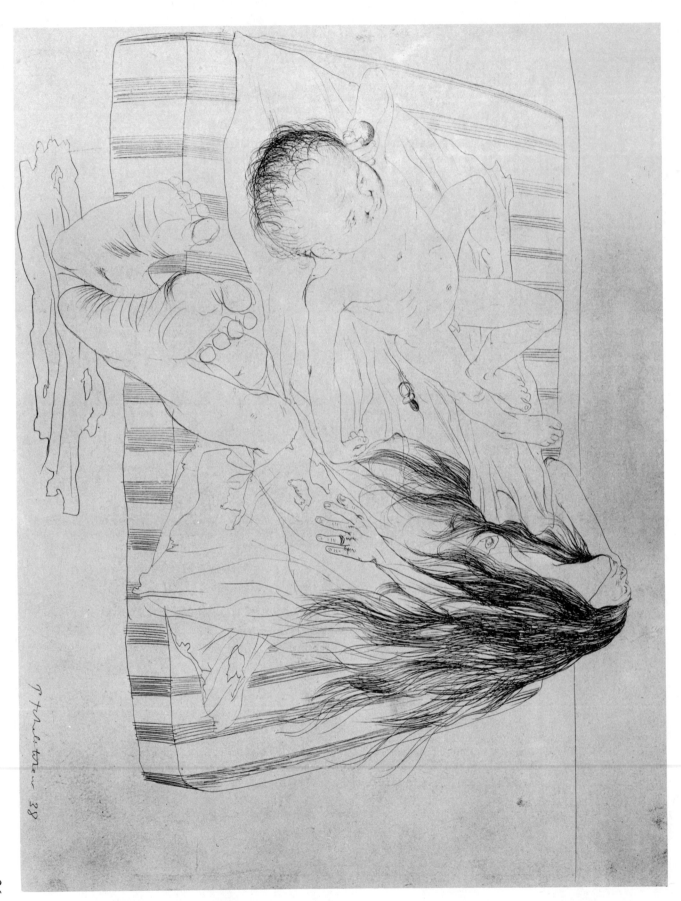

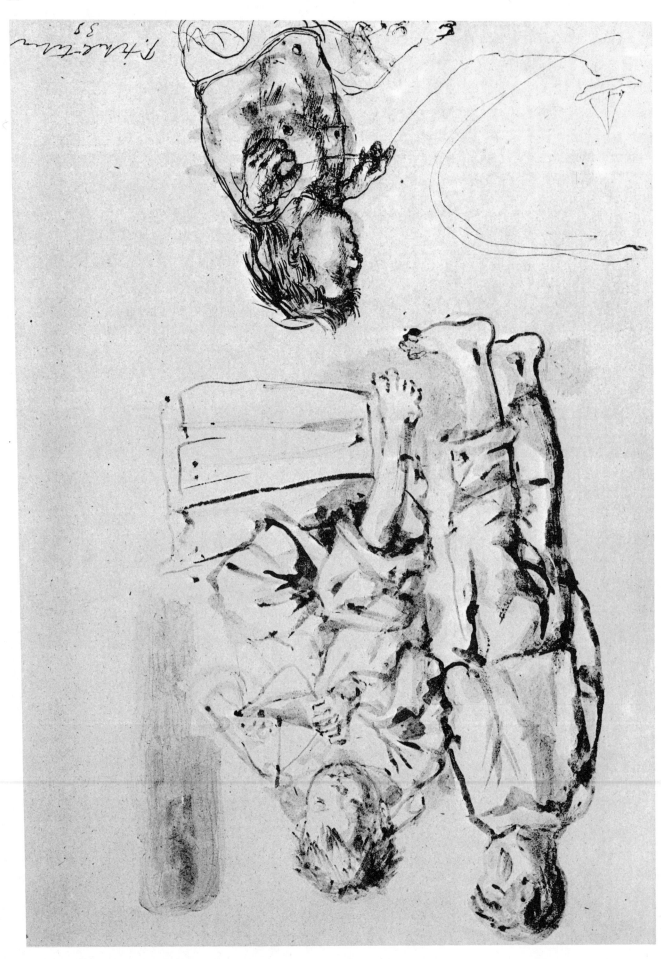

39

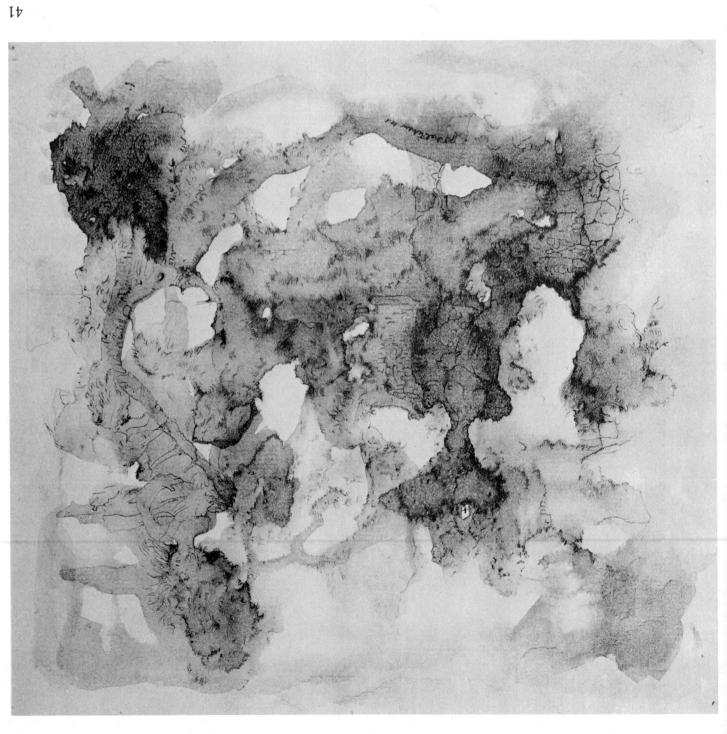

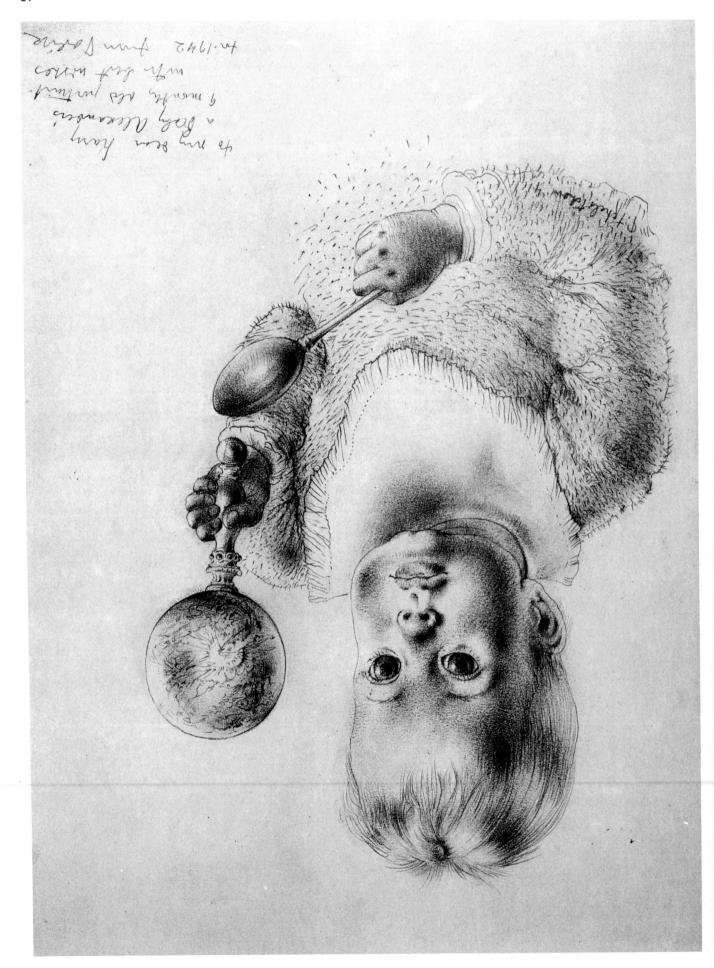

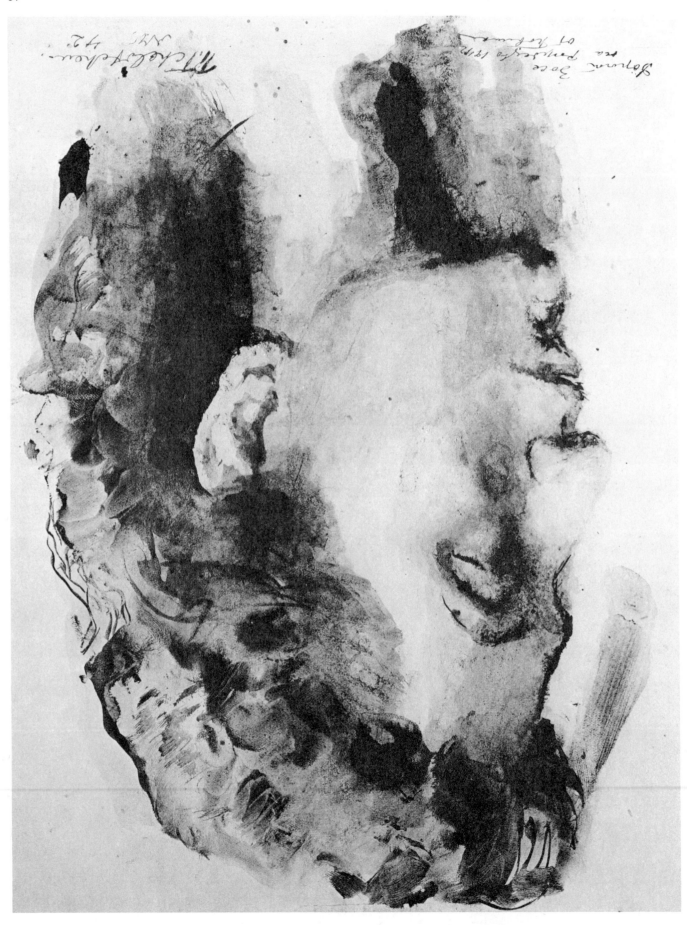

P. Tchelitchew
44

45

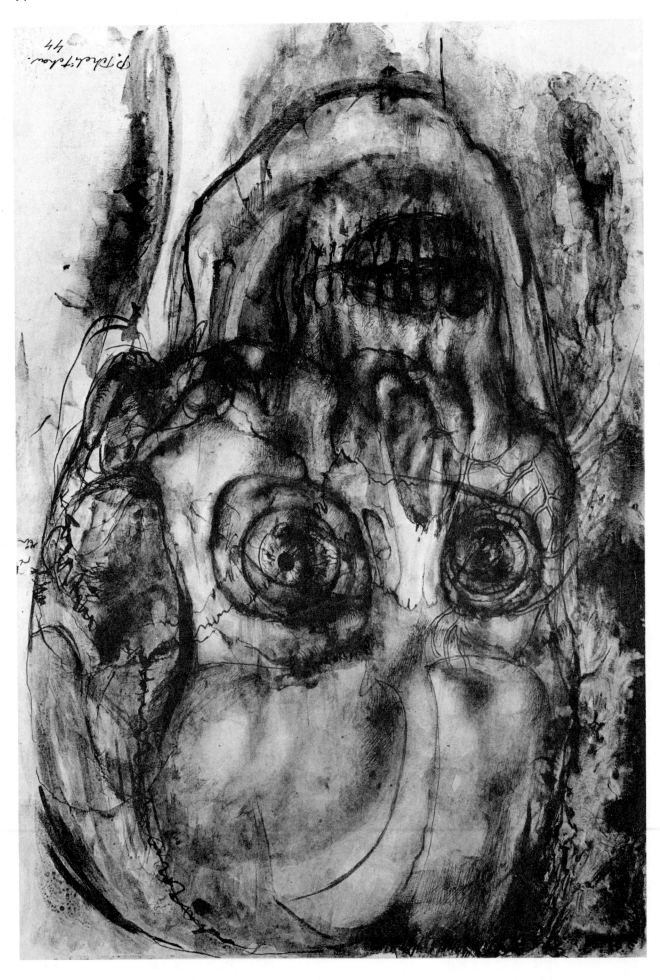

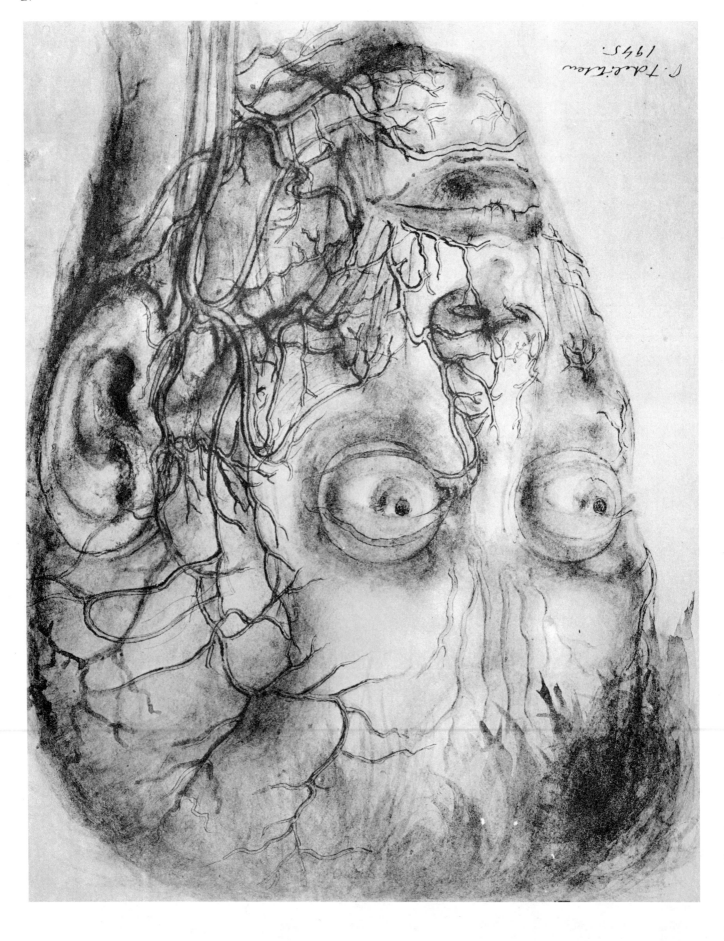

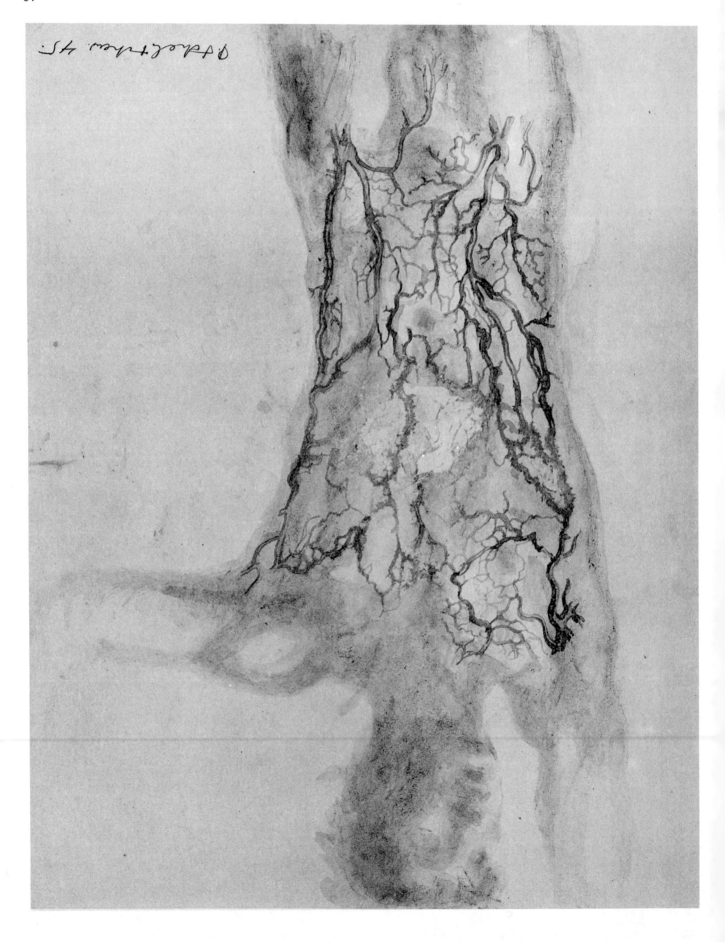